Editor
Jennifer Overend Prior, Ph.D.

Managing Editor
Ina Massler Levin, M.A.

Editor-in-Chief
Sharon Coan, M.S. Ed.

Illustrators
Renée Christine Yates
Bruce Hedges

Cover Artist
Lesley Palmer

Art Coordinator
Kevin Barnes

Art Director
CJae Froshay

Imaging
Temo Parra
Rosa C. See

Product Manager
Phil Garcia

Publishers
Rachelle Cracchiolo, M.S. Ed.
Mary Dupuy Smith, M.S. Ed.

A Year of
MATH

GRADES 1 - 2

Author

Sarah Kartchner Clark, M.A.

Teacher Created Materials, Inc.
6421 Industry Way
Westminster, CA 92683
www.teachercreated.com
ISBN-0-7439-3713-9
©2004 Teacher Created Materials, Inc.
Made in U.S.A.

Table of Contents

Introduction

With all the demands of our world, literacy is becoming increasingly vital. Though "literacy" is an often-used word in education today, many children in the world are growing up without a strong literacy foundation. Just what is literacy? The dictionary states that a literate person is one who is able to read and write.

The purpose of *A Year of Themes: Math* is to provide a literacy-rich environment in which children learn to use and enjoy written and spoken language and see their connection to math. The children will become immersed in print and use their developing language and math skills in purposeful activities. Students will learn phonetic sounds, hear rhyme and rhythm, and begin to understand language structure and mathematical concepts. *A Year of Themes: Math* contains familiar stories and rhymes to set a comfortable tone and create a familiar environment for the student.

This book has been divided into nine units—one for each month of the traditional school year. Each segment is based on a theme and has a literature selection and a mathematical focus. Each segment in this book is organized to include some or all of the following activities:

- lesson plans
- reproducible little books
- related literature suggestions
- math games
- word problems
- group discussion
- learning centers
- art projects
- math activities
- story-related visual aids
- journal writing ideas
- drama activities
- exposure to nonfiction text
- problem solving

Mathematics Standards and Objectives

All educators should be accountable for teaching skills and objectives that will promote math and literacy. Listed below are the objectives and skills that are taught in this book.

- Develop an understanding of number meaning.
- Demonstrate a one-to-one correspondence between elements in collections.
- Use manipulatives to count, order, and group.
- Recognize relationships between concrete representations, number names, and representations of numbers.
- Compare and sort objects by their physical attributes.
- Collect, organize, and describe simple data.
- Using concrete objects, create, describe, and extend a variety of patterns.
- Recognize geometry in surroundings.
- Recognize that a single object has different attributes (texture, size, color, length, etc.)
- Compare and order objects according to attributes.
- Use a variety of puzzles and games involving counting problems.

A Year of Themes in Math

This book is divided into nine segments providing you with a different theme and literature selection for each month of the traditional school year. Use the themes to teach skills and information and use the literature selections to teach literacy and mathematical concepts. Here is a suggested outline:

September—Apples, Apples, Apples

The theme this month is "Apples, Apples, Apples." Use "The Apple Tree" little book as an opportunity to practice counting. This book lends itself to a discussion about apples this time of year and what can be done with apples. Use this unit to teach counting from one to five.

October—Halloween Happenings

October is a good time to use "Halloween Happenings" as a theme to teach your students about these fall traditions. "Five Little Pumpkins" shares the experience of five pumpkins on Halloween. Use this unit to introduce ordinal numbers.

November—Our Wonderful World

Autumn brings the change of colors and the crisp, cool, air. It's the perfect time to be outside and explore the world. Use the story "Shapes, Shapes, Everywhere" to start your exploration. Students will be able to locate shapes in their world. Use this unit to teach and locate shapes.

December—Winter Is Here!

The "Winter is Here!" theme lends itself easily to gearing up for the exciting days ahead. The "Ten Little Snowflakes" little book adds to the wonder of the season. Use this unit to introduce counting from one to ten and back again.

January—Getting Dressed All by Myself!

With the coming of snow and rain during the season, students have plenty of practice getting dressed and wearing lots of layers. The theme, "Getting Dressed All by Myself!" can teach buttoning, zipping, and tying skills to your students. Use the little book "One, Two, Buckle My Shoe" to teach the theme and to teach students counting from one to ten.

February—My Family

A favorite holiday this time of year is Valentine's Day. Use the little book "My Happy Family" to remind students of the important people in their life. This theme can assist you in teaching patterns. Students can make their own valentines to send to loved ones and to experiment with making patterns.

March—What Time Is It?

How much further? Are we there yet? Do these questions sound familiar? Use the little book "Hickory, Dickory, Dock" to teach the basics of telling time. Can students find the numbers on the clock? What do these numbers mean? This theme can help students become familiar with clocks and telling time.

April—Farm Animals

Have you ever visited a farm? What types of animals are found on a farm? Use this theme to teach about farm animals. Use the poem "Baa, Baa, Black Sheep" to teach beginning addition to your students.

May—Animals in Our World

The little book "Five Little Monkeys" lends itself easily to learning about the animals in our world. Where do animals live? What do they eat? Use this unit to teach beginning subtraction to your students.

Preparing this Math Literacy Unit

Encouraging literacy can be a continuous process filling every waking minute. Immersing your students in literacy and math activities can build a solid foundation for years to come. Listed below are activities and suggestions you can implement to make *A Year of Themes: Math* a success in your classroom.

Making the Little Books

There are nine well-known stories and poems used to teach literacy in this book. Each story or poem comes with little books for your students. Reproduce the pages of the little books. Books may be assembled before the lesson or students may help complete the following steps. (1) Cut on the lines. (2) Check to make sure the pages are in the correct order. (3) Then staple the pages together. Students may use crayons or colored pencils to color their little books. Be sure to allow time for students to read them independently, with partners, or as a class. When you have finished studying the books in class, send them home for students to share with their families.

Activity Pages

There are activity pages to go with each little book. These activity pages are used to give students practice in reading, writing, counting, and solving problems. Reproduce the activity pages for the students as needed. Directions for using the pages are provided in the lesson plans. You will find pages introducing the math focus for that unit. This book also provides a variety of math games to play with students to reinforce math concepts being taught in the unit. You can choose to play these games in small groups, with partners, or as a whole class. Be sure to vary the type of group to allow all students an opportunity to play and practice math skills.

Problem-of-the-Day

Begin each day solving a problem together as a class. These problems can incorporate simple math skills such as counting, telling time, finding patterns, measuring, adding and subtracting, and solving story problems. Use the names of students in your class to call interest to the problems.

Word Wall

Set aside a place in your classroom to write down easy-to-read, common words that are found in the little books. Be sure to include mathematical words and phrases on this word wall. Some math words include greater than, less than, equal, bigger, smaller, straight, circle, square, triangle, rectangle, and diamond. Take time to allow students to practice reading these words before, during, and after they read the little books. Encourage students to add words to the word wall.

Calendar Activities

Use the daily calendar as an opportunity to teach math skills. The calendar can lend itself to math and literacy activities such as, writing the number of days school has been in session, making patterns on the calendar, counting by twos, fives, and tens, using tally marks, grouping, regrouping, and taking away.

The Apple Tree

Way up high in the apple tree,

Five red apples smiled at me.

I shook that tree as hard as I could.

Down came the apples,

And mmmm, they were good!

6

The Apple Tree Lesson Plans

Week One

1. Draw a picture of an apple on the chalkboard. Ask students to tell you what color to draw the apple. There will be some disagreement as apples come in different colors. Share a variety of apples with the students. Discuss how they grow. Do they grow in the ground? on a bush? on a tree? Next ask students what apples taste like. Allow time for students to share ideas. Display the little book "The Apple Tree." Explain to students that you are going to read a poem about five apples up in an apple tree.

2. Read the poem "The Apple Tree." You may copy and enlarge page 6 to use for this activity. Be sure to read the poem two or three times. As you read the poem aloud, encourage your students to join in when they can. Point to each word as you read it.

3. Discuss with students why the tree was shaken. What would be another way to get the apples down? Ask students to share experiences they have had with picking apples or climbing apple trees.

4. Distribute copies of "The Apple Tree" little book. Have students color the pages and then cut them out. Help students assemble and staple their books together. Divide students into pairs and have them read their little books together.

Week Two

1. The focus for this little book is counting from one to five. Discuss the numbers one through five with students. Write each of the numbers on the chalkboard and have students repeat the numbers as you write them. Next, ask one student at a time to come up and point to a given number. (For example, you may say, "Please point to the number two.") Then have each student close his or her eyes and hold up one finger. Explain to the students that this is a magic finger and you will be asking their magic fingers to write numbers in the sky. Now call out a number and have the students use their magic fingers to write the number. You can also have students call out numbers and check to be sure that they are "writing" the number correctly. Next, have students complete page 12.

2. Read "The Apple Tree" aloud to students from a little book like theirs. Have students follow along in their little books as you read. Point to each word as you read it. After reading the story, have students look for words. Write the word *apples* on the chalkboard and see if students can find and point to the word. Other words to look for are *tree, high, hard, five, down, good.* Discuss how illustrations and pictures can help them locate words.

3. Arrange to make one of the apple recipes on page 13. The recipes are for applesauce or apple tarts. Making these recipes will give students hands-on experience with apples and measurement. The applesauce is an easier recipe, but uses fewer measuring skills. Be sure to involve your students in the measuring/cooking process and to have plenty of parent help on hand.

The Apple Tree Lesson Plans *(cont.)*

Week Three

1. Explain to students that learning to count is important. Knowing how to use numbers can help them to be successful in life. Make up a word problem using the students in your class and see if they can solve the problems. For example, "Jane shook the apple tree and four apples fell down." (Draw the four apples on the chalkboard.) "As she walked away, another apple fell down from the tree." (Draw another apple next to the original four.) Ask students to tell you how many apples are now on the ground. Count the apples with the students by pointing to each one as you say the number. There were five apples on the ground. Next, enlist the help of your students to make up a word problem using apples and the numbers one through five. Solve the problem as a class. Now working as a class, read and solve the word problems on page 14.

2. Read "The Apple Tree" to the students from their little books on a story chart. Now read a different story that has counting apples or counting to five in the story. (See the bibliography on page 96.) Discuss the similarities and differences between each story. If time allows, have students act out the stories as you read them. When finished, have students count the apples or count the numbers in the story. Practice counting from one to five with students.

3. Write the poem on sentence strips. Post the sentence strips out of order on the chalkboard. Have students assist you in placing the strips in order. Read the sentences again to check the sequence. Make changes as needed.

4. Read the story again with the students while they follow along in their little books. Point to each word as you read it, but this time, do not say all the words. Point to a word without reading it and have students read it for you. Allow students to do more and more of the reading each time.

5. As an art activity, supply students with green, brown, and white construction paper and five red puff balls. The white paper is used as the background. The green and brown paper is used to make the tree. Students count out five red puff balls and glue them on the tree as apples. They can glue some apples on the tree and some on the ground. Allow time for students to share their pictures and count the apples.

Week Four

1. Share a story about apples or a story that has apples in it. (See bibliography page 96.) Discuss the differences between the story and the apple poem. Count the apples in the story. Have children dictate a story that uses five objects. Write the stories and have students draw the pictures. Have a sharing time for students to share their stories. Make covers for these little books and store them in the class library.

2. Go on a scavenger hunt looking for groups of five in the classroom or around the school. Have students share their findings with each other. If you have apple trees close to your school, you could take students to count the apples on the tree.

3. As your concluding activity for this unit, play the games on page 15. These games will give students practice counting to five and hearing others count to five. Spend time each day counting with your class. The more students count and write numbers, the firmer their understanding of numbers will be.

Math Literacy in the Works

This page features learning-center suggestions that can be used to reinforce skills taught and discussed in the classroom. Select the centers that will best meet the needs of your students.

Math Center

- Have a wide variety of counting materials available. Have students categorize each of these items into groups of five.
- Make pre-cut stamps out of apples. The stamps can be any design such as stars, squares, circles, etc. Using paint, students can stamp five stars, five circles, five squares, etc., or they can paint a pattern using the apple stamps.

Reading Center

- Set up an area in your room for independent reading. Provide beanbags, pillows, or chairs for more comfort. Keep a shelf of books available at all times for students to read and browse. For this center, have counting books available for students to count and read. (See the bibliography on page 96.)
- Have sentence strips containing the lines from the "The Apple Tree" story. At this center, have students work together to read the sentences and figure out the sequence of the story. Have a little book of this story available for students to check their work or to use as needed.

Writing Center

- Have paper and writing utensils available for each student to create or share a recipe for his or her favorite apple dish. Students should use inventive spelling to write the recipes. What do they think are the ingredients to put in the apple dishes? How many apples are used? Is the dish cooked? If so, at what temperature should this dish be baked in the oven? How many does this recipe serve? Compile all of these recipes to create an apple cookbook.

Art Center

- Set up an easel with paper. Have students use watercolor paints to paint pictures of the five apples in the tree and on the ground. Students may paint the different phases in the story. Hang the paintings around the room when they are dry.

Science Center

- Display nonfiction books, magazine articles, and posters about apples. Have students browse these materials to learn more. Arrange a time in the day to have students report to the class what they have learned about apples and how they are used.

Dramatic Play Center

- Using felt, cut out trunks, tree tops, and five small red apples. Have students repeat "The Apple Tree" poem using the felt pieces.

Making the Little Book

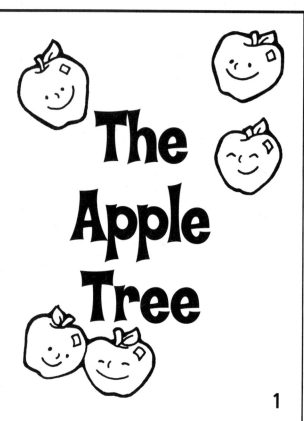

The Apple Tree

1

Way up high in the apple tree, 2

Five red apples smiled at me. 3

I shook the tree as hard as I could, 4

10

Making the Little Book *(cont.)*

Down came the apples,

5

and mmmm, they were good!

6

1
2
3
4
5

7

The End

8

Counting to Five

There were five apples that fell from the apple tree. Can you count to five?
Count the apples in each row and write the number on the line.

1.   _____

2.   _____

3.   _____

4.   _____

5.   _____

A is for Apples

There are many things you can do with apples. Apples come in a variety of colors and sizes. Get out your measuring spoons and select the recipe that you would like to try!

Crock Pot Applesauce

This recipe will feed your whole class! Check for allergies before serving.

Ingredients

- ten cooking apples, cored and diced (any kind, peel on)
- ¼ cup (60 mL) water
- ½ cup (120 mL) sugar
- cinnamon, to taste
- 1 tablespoon (15 mL) butter or margarine (optional)

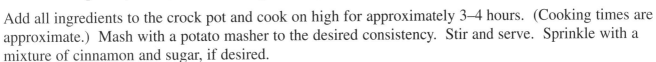

Add all ingredients to the crock pot and cook on high for approximately 3–4 hours. (Cooking times are approximate.) Mash with a potato masher to the desired consistency. Stir and serve. Sprinkle with a mixture of cinnamon and sugar, if desired.

Apple Tarts

Serves 8. Check for allergies before serving.

Ingredients

- 6 tablespoons (90 mL) butter, cut into small pieces
- 1½ cups (360 mL) plus 2 tablespoons (30 mL) all-purpose flour
- 4 tablespoons (60 mL) cold water
- 3 tablespoons (45 mL) sugar
- 2 pounds (.9 kg) apples, cored and diced

Directions

1. With a fork or pastry blender, combine 1½ cups of flour, water, and butter. Mix to form a ball.

2. Using a rolling pin, roll out the dough into a circle about 13 inches (32.5 cm) in diameter and about ¼" (.6 cm) in thickness.

3. Pick up the dough and place it over a 10½" (26.8 cm) tart pan. (A pie pan can be substituted.) Press the dough gently into the pan and refrigerate for 15 minutes. Preheat the oven to 375°F (190°C).

4. Blend the 2 tablespoons of flour with 1 tablespoon of the sugar. Sprinkle the bottom of the tart shell evenly with the flour mixture. Place the diced apples into the shell. Sprinkle the apples with the remaining sugar and bake on the bottom rack of the oven for 45 minutes. Enjoy!

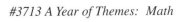

Math in the Real World

Everyday we use math. Work as a class or in small groups to solve these math problems about apples and apple trees.

❶ Sally and Fran wanted to climb the apple tree after school. They ran to the backyard. Both were soon climbing the tree. How many girls are climbing the apple tree?	**❷** Read the little book titled "The Apple Tree." Look at the picture on page 3 in the book. How many apples are in the tree? _____
❸ An apple tree was growing by the school yard. The wind knocked six apples off the tree. They fell on the ground. Draw six apples.	**❹** Mr. Jones grows apple trees in his backyard. One of the trees has red apples, one has green apples, and one has yellow apples on it. How many apple trees does Mr. Jones have?

❺ Draw an apple tree that has five apples on it. What color are your apples?

- -

Fold under before reproducing.

Answers: 1. Two girls. 2. There are five apples in the tree. 3. Students should draw six apples. 4. Mr. Jones has three apple trees. 5. Students should draw a tree with five apples on it.

Counting Math Games

Games are a fun way to learn math. Play these games with partners, in groups, or as a class.

The Last One Standing

Directions:

1. Have all the students stand in a circle.

2. Each student says a number as the class counts to five. The first student says, "one." The second says, "two," and play continues this way around the circle. The student that says the number five has to sit down. Play continues with students who say the number five sitting down.

3. The last student standing is the winner.

Toss to Five

Directions:

1. Have your students sit in a circle.

2. Using a lightweight ball or bean bag, take turns tossing it from student to student. Each time a student throws the ball, he or she calls out a number.

3. The students continue counting to five while tossing the ball. You can increase the number students count to if they have mastered counting to five.

4. A variation of this game would be to toss and catch the ball and count how many catches your class can do without dropping the ball. Counting begins again each time the ball is dropped.

Five Little Pumpkins

Five little pumpkins sitting on a gate.

The first one said, "My, it's getting late."

The second one said,
"There are witches in the air."

The third one said, "But we don't care."

The fourth one said, "Let's run and run."

The fifth one said,
"Isn't Halloween fun?"

Then oooo went the wind
and out went the lights,

And five little pumpkins
rolled out of sight.

Five Little Pumpkin Lesson Plans

Week One

1. On the chalkboard, draw three columns. In the first column, list all the information that students already know about pumpkins. In the second column, list questions that students have about pumpkins. At the end of the lesson, record in the third column the information that students have learned.

2. Bring five pumpkins for students to observe. Have students share observations with one another about what they notice about each of the pumpkins. What color is a pumpkin? What do students think a pumpkin feels like? What does a pumpkin look like on the inside? What types of things can you do with a pumpkin? Place the pumpkins in a line. Now ask students which pumpkin is first? Which pumpkin is in line second? third? fourth? fifth?

3. Explain to students that you are going to read a poem about five little pumpkins. Write the poem on page 16 on chart paper and then read it aloud. What happens to the pumpkins? What holiday is mentioned in this poem? What does a pumpkin have to do with Halloween?

4. Distribute copies of the little book "Five Little Pumpkins." Have students color the pages and cut them out. Help students assemble and staple their books together. Pair students with partners and have them read their little books together.

Week Two

1. The focus for this little book is to identify and understand ordinal numbers. Discuss the numbers one through five with your students. Write each of the numbers on the chalkboard and have the students repeat them as you write. Next, write the words *first, second, third, fourth,* and *fifth* on the chalkboard. Ask students to help you match up the numeral with the ordinal number word. Next, arrange a group of students in a line. Ask the class to identify the first student in the line. Then, find the second student, third student, fourth student, and fifth student. Have students complete page 22 about ordinal numbers one through five.

2. Read "Five Little Pumpkins" aloud to students from a little book like theirs. Have them follow along in their little books. Point to each word as you read it. After reading the story, have students look for words. Write the word *pumpkin* on the chalkboard and ask students to find and point to the word. Other words to look for are *Halloween, first, second, third, fourth,* and *fifth.* Distribute page 23 and have students follow the directions to color the pictures.

3. Have students retell the poem "Five Little Pumpkins" to check comprehension. Suggest an event that took place out of sequence, and have students correct your sequencing. Select five students to act out the poem as you read it aloud.

4. The next time you line up your class, set aside some time to identify the ordinal number of each student in line. For example, have students identify the first person in line, then the second person in line, etc. Continue in this manner until all students have been identified in their place in line. You can repeat this activity once each day. Be sure students are in a different place in line each time. Invite them to help you identify the place of each student.

Five Little Pumpkins Lesson Plans (cont.)

Week Three

1. Read "Five Little Pumpkins" again with students. As the class reads, have five students dramatize the poem. Have each student act out what each pumpkin does.

2. Make pumpkins out of construction paper and give one to each student. Using a black marker or a black crayon, have each student design a face for the pumpkin. Divide students into groups of five to act out the story as they read it from their little books. Next, have each group hold up its pumpkins and stand in a line. Ask the first student in each line to raise his or her hand. Then ask for the third student to do the same. Once students become familiar with this process, speed it up. Call out ordinal numbers. The students in line raise their hands quickly when their ordinal numbers are called.

3. Read other stories that use ordinal numbers (See the bibliography on page 96) and other stories about pumpkins to your students. Discuss these stories and count the objects mentioned in each story.

4. Read the poem again with the students while they follow along in their little books. Point to each word as you read it, but this time, do not say all the words. Point to a word without reading it and have students read it. Allow students to do more and more of the reading each time.

5. Using the construction paper pumpkins made previously, have students act out math word problems. For example, have three students and their pumpkins line up in a straight line. Select one of the students to represent a brave pumpkin. Tell the class, "On Halloween night, there were three pumpkins. They wanted to go trick or treating. Two of the pumpkins were afraid. One was brave. So the brave one went first and the other two followed." Have students locate the first, second, and third pumpkins. For more practice with ordinal numbers and word problems, see page 24.

Week Four

1. Discuss whether the pumpkins in the story are real or make-believe characters. How can you tell? Allow time for students to explain their answers. Bring in a collection of posters, books, and magazine pictures that feature pictures or stories about pumpkins. Ask students to share their favorite activities with pumpkins and Halloween.

2. On the chalkboard write, "The pumpkin said…." Then have students copy these words and add an ending to the sentence. Remind them to write a period at the end of the sentence. Provide crayons or colored pencils and have them illustrate their sentences. Have a sharing time for students to share their sentences. Bind student pages together to create a book. Make a cover for this book and store it in the class library. Be sure to read the story aloud with students.

3. Give each student a piece of blank paper. Next, have students follow your directions. Your directions might be something like this: "First draw a circle at the top of the page. Second, draw a square at the bottom. The third thing I want you to do is draw a rectangle in the middle…." Continue with a fourth and fifth direction.

4. As a concluding activity, play math games to practice using ordinal numbers. Use the game suggestions on page 25 or use some of your own.

Math Literacy in the Works

This page features learning-center suggestions that can be used to reinforce skills taught and discussed in the classroom. Select the centers that will best meet the needs of your students.

Math Center

- Have each student draw pictures of pumpkins on a sheet of paper. When finished, have each student count all the pumpkins on this page and write the number at the top of the page.

- Cut out five pumpkins and write the corresponding ordinal numbers on each. When students come to this center, have them place the pumpkins in correct order. (i.e., first through fifth.)

Science Center

- Have students go with an adult on a search of real and make-believe pumpkins. (There should be plenty of Halloween decorations on display for this counting activity.) Display nonfiction books, magazine articles, and posters about pumpkins. Have students browse these materials to learn more about pumpkins. Designate a time in the day to have students report to the class about what they have learned about pumpkins.

- Have on display a pumpkin that is cut open. With adult supervision, allow students to explore the inside of a pumpkin. (Be sure to have this pumpkin sitting on plenty of newspaper.) Using their fingers, students point to the first pumpkin seed they see, the second pumpkin seed, and so forth. For close-up observations, have them use magnifying glasses. Have students quietly discuss and observe the pumpkin with other classmates at this center. What information can they gather from their observations? Why are pumpkins used at Halloween time?

Reading Center

- Have a variety of Halloween books available for students to look at and read. See if students can locate pumpkins in the book. How many pumpkins are in these stories?

Art Center

- Have a student paint a paper plate with orange tempera paint. Supply black construction paper and scissors for students to cut out jack-o'-lantern eyes and a mouth to glue onto the plate.

- Cut pictures from magazines that show sequence. Have students place the pictures in order. What happens first? second? third? fourth? fifth? Students can draw their own sequence pictures of events that took place before or after school.

Writing Center

- Supply paper, crayons, and other materials needed for students to write poems about pumpkins. They may draw pictures in place of words if necessary. Post the chart of the "Five Little Pumpkins" poem at this center. Students may use the poem as a guide.

Making the Little Book

Five Little Pumpkins

1

Five little pumpkins sitting on a gate. 2

The first one said, "My, it's getting late." 3

The second one said, "There are witches in the air." 4

Making the Little Book (cont.)

The third one said,
"But we don't care."   5

The fourth one said,
"Let's run and run."   6

The fifth one said,
"Isn't Halloween
fun?"   7

Then oooo went the
wind and out went
the lights,

And five little
pumpkins rolled out
of sight.   8

Ordinal Numbers

Draw a line to match each number on the left with the ordinal number on the right.

1   second

3   fifth

5   first

2   fourth

4   third

Draw a line of pumpkins. Write the ordinal number under each pumpkin.

Ordinal Numbers (cont.)

Follow the directions to color the pictures below.

1. Color the first child blue.

2. Color the fourth child green.

3. Color the second child red.

4. Color the fifth child yellow.

5. Color the third child purple.

Answer these questions

1. Is the fourth child a girl or a boy? _____

2. What is the second child holding in her hand? _____

3. What is the fifth child doing? _____

4. What do you think happened to the third child? _____

5. Is the first child a boy or a girl? _____

6. How many girls and how many boys are in this line? _____

Math in the Real World

Every day we use math. Work as a class or in small groups to solve these math problems about pumpkins and Halloween.

---

❶ Greg, Emily, and Anne are picking pumpkins so each can make a jack-o'-lantern. If they each want one, how many pumpkins do they need?

❷ On Halloween night, Jason counted all of the pumpkins in his neighborhood. He counted six on one street and two on the next street. How many pumpkins did Jason count all together?

❸ There are three pumpkins sitting on a porch. One pumpkin has a scary face. The others have happy faces. How many pumpkins have happy faces?

❹ Mrs. Smith grows pumpkins in a pumpkin patch to make pies. Mrs. Smith has picked the pumpkins below. Count them and write the number here: _____

---

❺ Draw a pumpkin patch that has five pumpkins in it.

Fold under before reproducing.

Answers: 1. Three pumpkins. 2. Jason counted eight pumpkins. 3. Two pumpkins have happy faces. 4. There are four.

     24

Math Counting Games

Games are a fun way to learn math. Play these games with partners, in groups, or as a class.

Who's on First?

Materials

- five pennies per student
- dried pumpkin seeds (optional)

Directions

1. Divide your class into groups of three or four. Designate one person in each group to be the "caller." Have students put their pennies in a straight line. (To keep with the Halloween theme, you may wish to use pumpkin seeds instead of pennies.) Have students identify which of their pennies is first, second, third, fourth, and fifth in line. (If you feel your students are ready, you can extend the ordinal numbers up to tenth. If you do, be sure each student has ten pennies.)

2. The caller then says an ordinal number from first through fifth. The student must then point to the correct penny to match the ordinal number that is called. When students are ready, have them increase the speed of the game. See who can keep up with the quick directions.

3. Have students rotate the role of caller to give each student in the group a turn.

The Last One!

Materials

- twenty-five pennies
- dried pumpkin seeds (optional)

Directions

1. Divide students into groups of two or three. Give each group a set of twenty-five pennies. (To keep with the Halloween theme, you may wish to use pumpkin seeds instead of pennies.) Place the pennies in the center of a table or desk.

2. Take turns removing the pennies from the pile. A student can take one, two, or three pennies at a time. Each time a penny is taken, the student must say the number of pennies he or she is taking. A student can take a different amount of pennies on each turn.

3. The student who ends up taking the last penny is the winner.

4. You can change this game by changing the number of pennies in the pile, or the number of pennies taken each time. The person who ends up with the last penny could also be the loser. Work with students to make up your own class rules for this game.

Shapes, Shapes, Everywhere!

I can see shapes everywhere.

I can see a circle.

I can see a rectangle.

I can see a square.

I can see a triangle.

I can see a diamond.

What a wonderful world!

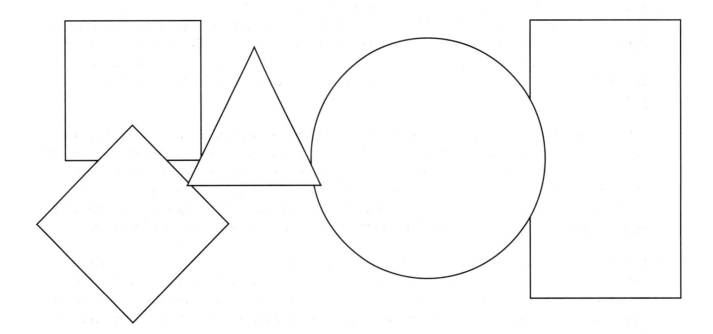

Can you find the diamond? the square? the circle? the rectangle? the triangle?

Shapes, Shapes, Everywhere! Lesson Plans

Week One

1. Prior to the lesson, cut out a diamond, triangle, square, circle, and rectangle using construction paper. Have your class identify each shape. Then hold up a shape and ask students to locate something in the classroom that is the same as the shape you are holding up. Make an enlarged copy of the shape story on page 26. After reading it aloud, ask students to identify the shapes on the page.

2. Explain that we live in a wonderful world. Tell students that you would like to explore the shapes that are found in the world. Go on a scavenger hunt with students to look for specific shapes. It is fun to locate shapes in nature. Keep track of the number of each type of shape found. Which shape was found the most?

3. Distribute copies of the little book "Shapes, Shapes, Everywhere." Have students color the pages and cut them out. Help them assemble and staple their books together. Pair students with partners and have them read their little books together.

Week Two

1. The focus for this little book is identifying and locating shapes. Discuss the different types of shapes with students. You may choose to talk about other shapes, such as the oval, that are not in the little book. Draw a picture of each shape and have students identify it. Have students complete page 32 about drawing and identifying shapes.

2. Read "Shapes, Shapes, Everywhere" aloud to students from a little book like theirs. Have them follow along in their little books. Model how to point to each word as you read it. After reading the story, have them look for words. Write the word *circle* on the chalkboard and have students find and point to the word. Other words to look for are *square*, *triangle*, *diamond*, and *rectangle*. Discuss how illustrations and pictures can help students locate words. Have students complete page 33.

3. Write a story, as a class, using shapes. Hold up a circle. Ask students to help you write a page about a circle. Have a student create an illustration to go with the words on this page. Next, hold up a square. Ask your class to write a one-page story about the square. Have another student create an illustration to go with this page about the square. Continue in this manner until each of the shapes has a page written about it. Compile these pages together to make a book. Read the book together as a class. Keep this book in the class library so students can read it often.

4. Before class make a list of questions about the shapes story and write them on slips of paper. Place these slips in a bowl. Invite each student to select a slip of paper from the bowl. Help students read the questions about the story. Then have them answer the questions. They can ask classmates for help if needed. You can also have students write questions to be answered by the class.

Shapes, Shapes, Everywhere! Lesson Plans *(cont.)*

Week Three

1. Discuss things that can be done with shapes. What can you make with shapes? Give the students cutouts of a variety of shapes. Using the shapes, have them create pictures. A student can make a train, a house, or anything the imagination inspires. Allow time for students to share their pictures and for the class to locate the shapes that were used in each one.

2. Read "Shapes, Shapes, Everywhere" to the students from their little books or the story chart. Now read another story with shapes in it. (See the bibliography on page 96.) Discuss the similarities and differences between the two stories with shapes. Ask them if these stories are real or make-believe. Read other stories you can find that have shapes in them. Discuss whether these stories are real or make-believe.

3. Read the story again with the students while they follow along in their little books. Point to each word as you read it, but this time, do not say all the words. Point to a word without reading it and have students read it. Allow students to do more and more of the reading each time.

4. As an art activity, supply students with small shapes. Each student should then make a "shape buddy" by painting a design or a face on a circle. Other shapes can make the body parts of the shape buddy.

Week Four

1. Explain that shapes are a part of our world. As a class or in small groups, work through the math word problems on page 34. Encourage students to watch for shapes in their world.

2. Do a hands-on activity with your class. Make three or four large shapes out of boxes or bags. Bring these shapes to class and write numbers on the sides. Using a hula-hoop, have each student, in turn, aim for a shape and add up scores.

3. Provide students with sidewalk chalk and have them create designs using shapes. As an additional activity, call out directions for students such as, "Everyone find a circle to stand on" and "Now jump to a square."

4. Have students review shapes by using their "magic fingers" (see page 7, week 2, activity 1) to draw shapes in the air. Say the name of a shape. Have students close their eyes and make the shape in the air with their magic fingers. As you go through this activity, review characteristics of each shape to help prompt students to draw the shape. For example, you may say, "A square has four equal sides." "A triangle has three lines and three corners." "A circle has one curving line with no sides."

5. As your concluding activity for this unit, play the games on page 35. These games should be played in small groups or as a class.

Math Literacy in the Works

This page features learning-center suggestions that can be used to reinforce skills taught and discussed in the classroom. Select the centers that will best meet the needs of your students.

Math Center

- Distribute cutouts of different shapes. Have students categorize the shapes. Then have them count the groups. Which shape has the most cutouts? How many? Then write numbers on pieces of paper. A student selects a number and counts out that many shape cutouts and glues them to the paper.

- Have each student select a shape and identify objects in the room that have this shape. (For example, the clock has a circle in it. The door is a rectangle.) Have students record the shapes found in the classroom.

- Supply students at this center with pattern blocks. Have them make designs or patterns using shapes. Students can trace the pattern blocks to make their designs permanent. Supply them with crayons to color the shapes.

Reading Center

- Write the lines from "Shapes, Shapes, Everywhere" on sentence strips. At this center, have students work together to read the sentences and determine the sequence of the story. Which strip comes first? Which one comes next? Have a little book of this story available for students to check their work.

- Set up an area in your room for independent reading. Provide beanbags, chairs, pillows, or chairs for more comfort. Keep a shelf of books available at all times for students to read and browse. For this center, have books about shapes available. (See the bibliography on page 96 for suggestions.) These can be stories that have shapes in them or they can be nonfiction books about particular shapes and their characteristics.

Art Center

- Give each student a piece of white paper. Supply students with shapes of specific colors. For example, all the squares are red; all the circles are orange; all the triangles are yellow, etc. Have each student make a shape rainbow by arranging similar shapes in arches and gluing them down. Display the rainbows around the room.

Writing Center

- Fold a piece of white paper in half twice. Cut on the folds to make four pages. Staple the four pages together to make a book. Have each student each select a shape and write a story about the adventures of this little shape. Students should illustrate their shape stories.

Shapes, Shapes, Everywhere

1

I can see shapes everywhere.

2

I can see a circle.

3

I can see a rectangle.

4

Making the Little Book (cont.)

I can see a square.

5

I can see a triangle.

6

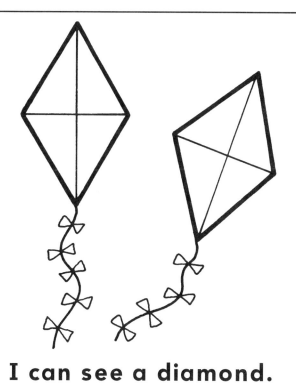

I can see a diamond.

7

What a wonderful world!

8

Making Shapes

Look at the shapes in each row. Look at the first shape. Trace the second shape in each row. Then make your own shape on the line.

1.

2.

3.

4.

5.

32

Shapes In Our World

Make a picture from each shape below. Draw your picture in the box below.

1.

2.

3.

4.

1.	2.
3.	4.

Math in the Real World

Every day we use math. Work as a class or in small groups to solve these math problems about shapes and our world.

❶ Elise and Tori are carrying round balloons. What shape are the balloons?	❷ Can you think of three things that are shaped like a square in the grocery store? Draw pictures of these items below.
❸ Draw a picture of something that has a diamond shape in it.	❹ Draw a triangle in this box. How many sides does a triangle have?

❺ Draw a shape that has four sides to it. What is the name of your shape?

Fold under before reproducing.

Answers: Answers: 1. The balloons are circles. 2. Answers will vary. 3. Answers will vary. 4. A triangle has three sides. 5. The shape is a diamond, a rectangle, or a square.

Math Games

Games are a fun way to learn math. Play these games with partners, in groups, or as a class.

Shape Scavenger Hunt

Materials

- clipboards with paper
- pencils

Directions

1. Divide your students into groups of two or three. Give each group a clipboard, a pencil, and paper.

2. Students are to look around the room to locate objects that have a specific shape. Students should record these objects on their clipboards. Set a specific amount of time that students have to locate the shapes. The group that finds the most items is the winning group.

Staying in Shape

Materials

- cutouts of circles, diamonds, rectangles, squares, and triangles

Directions

1. This game is played as a class and is best played outdoors. Give each student a shape to hold. Ask the students to sit in a large circle.

2. Explain that when you say the name of a given shape, all students holding that shape should stand up and run around the circle back to their original places.

3. Once you have named each shape, begin to combine shapes. For example, "All students holding squares and circles run around the circle."

4. As a variation, add colors to the mix. "Any student holding a red shape or a triangle can run around the circle."

5. Other variations to this game include skipping, galloping, walking, hopping, and jumping around the circle.

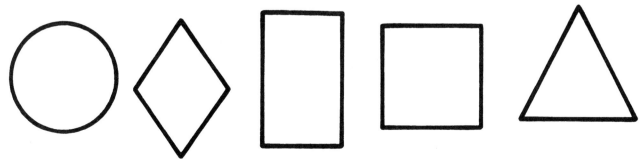

Ten Little Snowflakes

One little, two little, three little

 snowflakes,

Four little, five little, six little

 snowflakes,

Seven little, eight little, nine little

snowflakes,

Ten little snowflakes falling!

Ten Little Snowflakes Lesson Plans

Week One

1. Begin the unit by asking students to tell you their favorite things to do in the winter. How is winter different from the other seasons? Explain that you are going to read a poem about ten snowflakes. Have the students count to ten before reading the poem.

2. Prior to the lesson, copy the poem "Ten Little Snowflakes" (page 36) on chart paper. Read the story aloud. Encourage the students to join in on the repetitive parts of the poem. After finishing the poem, ask them to join you in reading the poem again.

3. Distribute copies of the little book "Ten Little Snowflakes." Have students color the pages and cut them out. Help them assemble and staple their books together. Pair students with partners and have them read their little books together.

4. The focus of this little book is counting from one to ten. Write each number on the chalkboard and point to it as students tell you the name of the number. Have the students complete page 42 about writing numbers from one to ten.

Week Two

1. Read "Ten Little Snowflakes" aloud from a little book. Have the students follow along in their little books. Point to each word as you read it. After reading the poem, have students look for words. Write the word *one* on the chalkboard and ask the students to find and point to the word. Other words to look for are *two*, *three*, *four*, *five*, *six*, *seven*, *eight*, *nine*, and *ten*. Discuss how these words are number words and represent numerals. Then have the students complete page 43, counting the number of snowflakes in each group.

2. Prior to class, write the numbers from 1–10 on index cards. Begin by having students count from one to ten. Next, distribute the index cards to ten students. Explain to the class that you would like students to line up in order from 1 to 10. Ask the student with card one to line up first. Continue in this manner until all students with cards are lined up from 1 to 10. Now distribute the cards again to different students. This time explain that you would like them to line up from ten to one.

3. Read "Ten Little Snowflakes" to the students. Prior to the reading, assign certain students to read specific pages of the book. As you go through the story, let students read their assigned pages. After reading the story, read other stories about counting to ten and about snowflakes. (See the bibliography on page 96 for suggestions.) Discuss what students have learned after reading books about snowflakes. You can have students count the number of snowflake pictures they find in the books about snowflakes.

Week Three

1. Discuss things that can be done with snow. (Snow can be used to build a snowman, construct a snow fort, to sled down, etc.) Ask students if it would be possible to count all the snowflakes that fall to the ground. Why or why not?

2. Make snowflakes out of felt material. Read "Ten Little Snowflakes" to the students from the story chart. Give each of ten students a felt snowflake to hold. Have them use the felt pieces to dramatize the poem about the ten snowflakes. Students should take turns placing their snowflakes on a flannel board.

3. Read the story again with the students while they follow along in their little books. Point to each word as you read it, but this time, do not say all the words. Point to a word without reading it and have students read it. Allow students to do more and more of the reading each time.

4. As an art activity, supply students with glue, waxed paper, and glitter. With the help of an adult, have each student design a snowflake by squeezing a thick trail of glue on the wax paper. Students should then sprinkle glitter atop the glue. Allow the glue to dry completely and then carefully peel the snowflake from the waxed paper. These sparkling snowflakes can be used to decorate your classroom. The students can also use them for counting practice.

Week Four

1. Explain to students that numbers are a part of our world. Work through the math word problems on page 44 about numbers and snowflakes as a class or in small groups. Encourage students to observe numbers in their world.

2. Help students make a counting book. Cut and staple pieces of paper together to make a little book with ten pages. Have each student write a different number from one to ten (in sequence) on each page. Next, the student draws a set of objects corresponding with the number on each page. Students can draw sets of snowflakes throughout the book or any objects they choose. When finished, have students read their counting books by saying each number and the name of the objects drawn. For example, "Two snowflakes."

3. Provide students with sidewalk chalk and have them practice writing their numbers. Students can also draw sets of objects to represent each number they write.

4. Have students review numbers by using their "magic fingers" to draw numbers in the air. Say numbers from one to ten. Have students close their eyes, and draw the numbers in the air with their fingers.

5. As a concluding activity for this unit, play the games on page 45. These games can be played in small groups or as a class.

Math Literacy in the Works

This page features learning-center suggestions that can be used to reinforce skills taught and discussed in the classroom. Select the centers that will best meet the needs of your students.

Math Center

- Provide manipulatives for students to count, sort, and group. Write numbers on index cards from one to ten (or higher). Students select number cards and count out corresponding sets of manipulatives. (Be sure to have higher numbers available for students who need a challenge.)

- Fill a jar with cotton balls or marshmallows. Have students write their predictions of how many cotton balls or marshmallows are in the jar. After all of the predictions have been made, count the contents of the jar with the whole class present.

Reading Center

- Set up an area in your room for independent reading. Provide large bean bags, pillows, or chairs for more comfort. Keep a bookshelf of books available at all times for students to read and browse. For this center, have different stories about snowflakes and counting from one to ten and beyond. (See the bibliography on page 96.)

Art Center

- Provide students with construction paper, crayons, glue and cotton balls. Have students color winter pictures, gluing on cotton balls for snow. Students might design snowflakes, snowmen, snow piles, snow forts, or other things made of snow.

- Provide students with white paper and scissors. Have an adult show the students how to fold and cut out snowflakes. Encourage the students to design and create their own unique snowflakes. Display them around the room. Encourage students to walk around the classroom, counting the snowflakes on display.

Writing Center

- Have students write winter day or snowflake stories. What happens in the story? Is this a true or make-believe story? How does the story end?

- Provide metal rings or shower hooks and index cards for each student. Punch a hole in each index card. Students write number words from the story on the cards and place them on the metal rings. Encourage the students to practice reading the words.

Dramatic Play Center

- Provide students with costumes and props appropriate for the story about the ten little snowflakes. Encourage them to work together to create and act out the story. You can set aside a time for students to present their plays to the class.

Ten Little Snowflakes

1

One little, two little, three little snowflakes, 2

Four little, five little, six little snowflakes, 3

Seven little, eight little, nine little snowflakes, 4

Making the Little Book (cont.)

Ten little snowflakes falling.

5

10, 9,

8, 7,

6 . . .

6

5, 4,

3, 2,

1!

7

The End

8

Counting to Ten

Count to ten and back again. Practice writing your numbers below. The first one has been done for you.

0   0   0   0   0   0   0   0   0   0

1   _____

2   _____

3   _____

4   _____

5   _____

6   _____

7   _____

8   _____

9   _____

10   _____

Snowflakes, Snowflakes, Snowflakes

Count the snowflakes in each row and write the number on the line.

1. ❄ ❄ ❄ ❄ ❄ ❄ _____

2. ❄ ❄ ❄ ❄ _____

3. ❄ ❄ ❄ ❄ ❄
   ❄ ❄ ❄ ❄ ❄ _____

4. ❄ ❄ ❄ _____

5. ❄ ❄ ❄ ❄
   ❄ ❄ ❄ _____

6. ❄ ❄ ❄ ❄ ❄ _____

Math in the Real World

Every day we use math. Work as a class or in small groups to solve these math problems about the numbers one through ten.

❶ On a snowy day, three snowflakes fell on Jake's nose. Five more fell on his hat. How many snowflakes fell on Jake?	**❷** Draw a snowflake that has six points.
❸ Mrs. Jones watched snowflakes. First she counted six snowflakes and then she counted three more. How many snowflakes did she count?	**❹** In the story, there were ten little snowflakes. Write the numbers one through ten.

❺ There are six snowflakes in your hair. There is one snowflake on your nose. There is one more snowflake on your eyelash. Draw the number of snowflakes found on you.

- -

Fold under before reproducing.

Answers: 1. Eight snowflakes. 2. Students will draw snowflakes with six points. 3. Nine snowflakes. 4. Students will write numbers from one to ten. 5. Eight snowflakes will be drawn.

44

Math Games

Games are a fun way to learn math. Play these games with partners, in groups, or as a class.

More or Less?

Materials

- a deck of playing cards for every two students (remove face cards)

Directions

1. Divide students into groups of two. Each group shuffles its deck of cards and places the cards facedown in a pile.
2. One person in each group draws a card and places it faceup. Then the other student draws a card and places it faceup. The student with the highest number gets to keep both cards. The student with the most cards at the end of the game wins.
3. As a variation of this game, play in the same manner, but the student with the lowest card gets to take the cards.

Pasta with Numbers

Materials

- construction paper
- a pair of dice for each group of students
- box of tube-shaped pasta

Directions

1. Divide students into groups of four or five. Distribute a sheet of paper to each student. Have one student in each group roll the dice. The student gathers the corresponding number of pasta pieces and uses them to make a shape.
2. The next student rolls the dice, takes the corresponding number of pasta pieces, and makes another shape.
3. Play continues in this manner for a designated period of time.

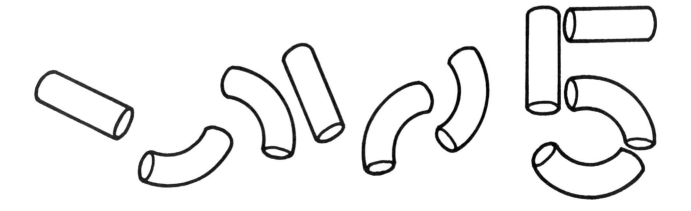

One, Two, Buckle My Shoe

One, two,
buckle my shoe.

Three, four,
shut the door.

Five, six,
pick up sticks.

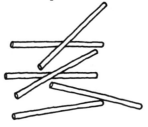

Seven, eight,
lay them straight.

Nine, ten,
now do it again.

One, Two, Buckle My Shoe Lesson Plans

Week One

1. Ask students if they know how to button their shirts, zip their pants and tie their shoes. Explain that these are all very important skills. Knowing how to get dressed by ourselves helps us to be independent. Explain that you have a poem about getting dressed and about being able to do things by ourselves. Display the poem (page 46) on chart paper. Ask some of these questions.

   - Can you tie your shoes?
   - Can you button your shirt and pants?
   - Can you zip your jacket?
   - Can you put on both socks?
   - When should you wear a hat?
   - When should you wear a coat?
   - What's the difference between a jacket and a coat?
   - Can you open and close an umbrella?

2. After you have read the poem, encourage the students to read it with you. Point to each word as you read it.

3. Discuss the verbs in this poem. Explain that this poem has many action words in it. See if students can find the verbs or action words. The first action word is *buckle*. What does buckle mean? Do all shoes buckle? What other action words help us fasten our shoes? (Suggestions might include zip, tie, and Velcro.) Identify other verbs in the poem, including *shut*, *pick up*, and *lay*. Read the poem again. As you read the poem, have students stand up and act out the verbs.

4. The focus of this little book is counting from one to ten. Write each number on the chalkboard and point to it as students tell you the name of the number. Have students complete page 52 for reinforcement of these numbers.

Week Two

1. Distribute copies of the little book poem. Have students color the pages and cut them out. Help them assemble and staple their books together. Pair students with partners and have them read their little books together.

2. Read "One, Two, Buckle My Shoe" aloud to students from a little book like theirs. Have students follow along in their little books. Point to each word as you read it. After reading the story, have students look for words. Write the word *buckle* on the chalkboard and see if students can find and point to the word. Other words to look for are: *one, two, door, sticks, three, four, straight, five, six, pick, seven, eight, again, nine,* and *ten*. Have students complete page 53 using number words from the poem.

3. Practice counting to ten with your class by playing the beanbag game. Have your class sit in a circle. One student has the beanbag and says "one." He or she then tosses the beanbag to another student and this student says, "two." Continue passing the beanbag with each student saying the next number. Speed up the game if desired. See how high the students can count without dropping the beanbag.

One, Two, Buckle My Shoe Lesson Plans *(cont.)*

Week Three

1. Read "One, Two, Buckle my Shoe" with the students. Then ask a student to read each page aloud while the other students follow along.

2. Write different lines of the poem on sentence strips. Post the sentence strips out of order on the chalk tray or in a pocket chart. Have students assist you in placing the strips in order. Read the sentences again to check the sequence. Have students make changes as needed. Try reading the poem with the sentence strips out of order. Can the students tell the correct order? (The rhyming words as well as the number sequence can help students put the poem in correct order.)

3. Discuss with students the importance of being able to dress themselves and do other important tasks. Allow time for students to practice zipping, buttoning, tying, and snapping. (Be sure to have necessary materials to practice these skills.) Next, create a cover for a big book entitled, "We Can Do It!" Have students draw pictures of things they can do all by themselves. Then have them write or dictate sentences to accompany their pictures. Bind all of these pages together in book. Be sure to share the book as a class and then store it in the class library for all students to read later.

Week Four

1. Read other stories with your class about doing things by themselves. You can refer to the bibliography on page 96 for suggestions. Go on a scavenger hunt in search of things that students can do independently in your classroom, on the playground, and around the school. (Skills might include sharpening their pencils, writing their names, opening and closing doors, getting a drink, taking the attendance sheet to the office, washing hands, using a swing correctly, etc.)

2. Read the poem again. Have a relay. Divide your class into groups of four or five. Students in each group form a line. Give each student in a group a different line from the poem to act out. For example, the first person in each line pretends to buckle his or her shoe. When finished, the second person pretends to shut a door. The third person pretends to pick up sticks and hands them to the next student. The fourth student puts the sticks in a straight line, and the fifth person says, "Do it again!" The first team to complete the tasks in the poem wins.

3. Have the students practice counting from one to ten by working through the word problems on page 54. Students can do these problems with partners or as a class. You may need to assist students in reading the problems.

4. As a concluding activity for this unit, have students work with partners or as a class to play the games on page 55. These games will give students more practice with counting and using numbers from one to ten.

Math Literacy in the Works

This page features learning-center suggestions that can be used to reinforce skills taught and discussed in the classroom. Select the centers that will best meet the needs of your students.

Math Center

- Provide discarded newspapers for students to browse through and cut up. Instruct students to find numbers in the newspapers to cut out and paste onto paper. As a variation, have students locate numbers in the newspaper and circle them using highlighter pens.

- Students work together at this center. The first student rolls a pair of dice, counts the dots on both dice, and chooses an activity for the group to perform, such as clapping. For example, if student rolls a four, he or she instructs the group to clap their hands four times. Play continues in this manner with students taking turns rolling the dice.

Reading Center

- Provide the students with the lines of the poem on sentence strips. Have students work together to read the sentences and determine the sequence of the poem. Have a little book of this story available for students to check their work.

- Set up an area in your room for independent reading. Provide large beanbags, pillows, or chairs for more comfort. Keep a bookshelf of books available at all times for students to read and browse. For this center, have versions of the counting books for students to read and count. (See the bibliography on page 96.)

Writing Center

- Ask each student to write about a personal experience with learning to do something all by himself or herself, such as riding a bike without training wheels or tying shoes for the first time. Have students write as many words as they can about their experiences. Then have students illustrate their experiences to provide more details.

- Provide students with clay and have students spell number words featured in the poem. Be sure to have the poem posted for student reference. Students may also practice making numerals from one to ten.

Art Center

- Have students color pictures of themselves getting dressed without help. When they have finished, cut the pictures into large puzzle pieces. Students can then try to put their puzzles back together again. Store the puzzles in envelopes so the pieces will not get lost.

One, Two, Buckle My Shoe

1

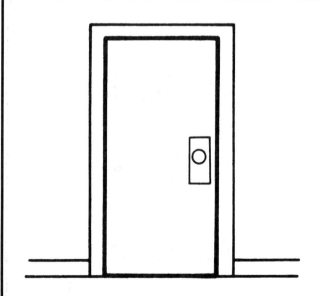

One, two, buckle my shoe.

2

Three, four, shut the door.

3

Five, six, pick up sticks.

4

Making the Little Book *(cont.)*

Seven, eight, lay them straight.   5

Nine, ten, do it again.   6

1, 2, 3,

4, 5, 6,

7, 8, 9,

10

7

10, 9, 8,

7, 6, 5,

4, 3, 2,

1

8

Counting to Ten

Draw a line from each group to its matching number.

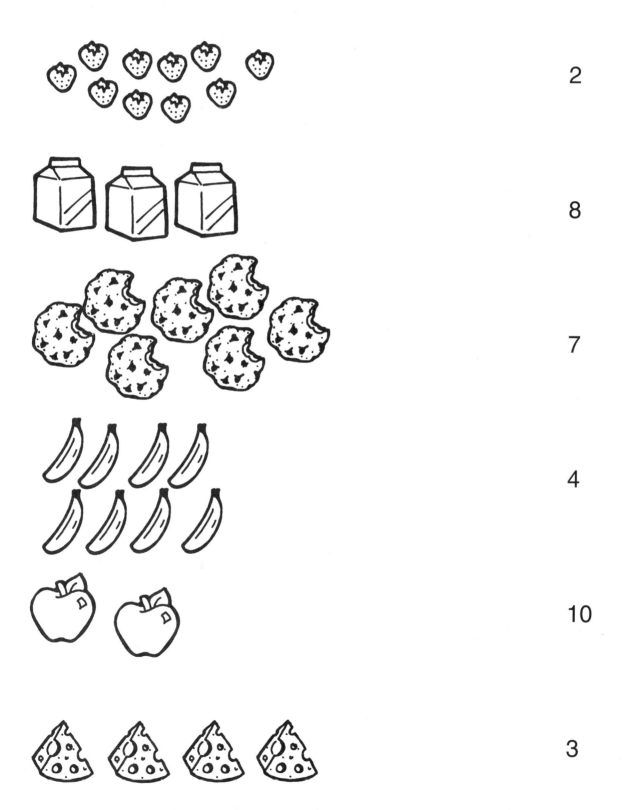

2

8

7

4

10

3

From One to Ten

Draw a line from each numeral to the matching number word.

1	One
2	Four
3	Nine
4	Six
5	Three
6	Ten
7	Eight
8	Five
9	Seven
10	Two

Math in the Real World

Every day we use math. Work as a class or in small groups to solve these math problems about the numbers one through ten.

❶ Six kids are putting their hats on before going out to recess. Draw six hats.

❷ Four girls and five boys are tying their shoes. How many kids all together are tying their shoes?

❸ There are six balls on the floor. There are four jump ropes on the floor, too. How many toys need to be picked up?

❹ In the story, there are six sticks. Draw six sticks in a straight line.

❺ There are four hats on your head. There is one hat on your nose. There is one more hat on your elbow. Draw the number of hats on you.

Fold under before reproducing.

Answers: 1. Student will draw six hats. 2. Nine kids are tying shoes. 3. There are ten toys to pick up. 4. Student will draw six sticks in a straight line. 5. There are six hats.

Math Games

Games are a fun way to learn math. Play these games with partners, in groups, or as a class.

Number Lotto

Materials

- a sheet of paper for each student (folded to make four sections)
- pencils
- ten index cards (numbered one through ten)
- four pennies for each student

Directions

1. Give each student a sheet of paper folded into fourths. Have each student choose four numbers between one and ten and write a number in each section of the paper using a pencil.

2. Distribute the pennies to each student to use as markers. Place the index cards face down in a pile.

3. Have students take turns selecting cards and calling out the numbers on the cards. If a student has this number on his or her paper, he or she places a penny on the number. The first player to place a penny on all four numbers is the winner.

4. Be sure to reshuffle the index cards at the beginning of each game. Between games, students can change the numbers they have on their papers if they want.

Number Art

Materials

- markers
- white construction paper for each student
- discarded magazines
- scissors
- glue or glue stick

Directions

1. Have each student select a number between one and ten. The student writes this number with a marker in the center of the construction paper. (Be sure the student writes this number in large print.)

2. The student then locates pictures of things he or she likes in magazines and cuts them out. When the student has found the same number of pictures as the number on the paper, he or she glues the pictures around the number on the construction paper. For example, if a student selected the number two, then the student would glue on two pictures.

My Happy Family

I love Mommy,
She loves me.
I love Daddy,
He loves me.
I love Sister,
She loves me.
I love Brother,
He loves me.
I love Grandma,
She loves me.
I love Grandpa,
He loves me.
I love my family!

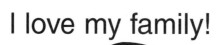

56

My Family Lesson Plans

Week One

1. Ask students to tell you about the members of their families. How do they feel about their families? Tell them that you have a poem about families. Read the poem "My Happy Family." You may copy and enlarge page 56 to use for this activity, if desired.

2. Read the poem again. When finished, ask students to name the members of the family mentioned in this story. There is a mom, a dad, a sister, a brother, a grandma, and a grandpa.

3. Point out to the students that there is a pattern in this poem. Write the poem on page 56 on chart paper and have your students look for a pattern.

4. Since this month is February, provide materials that students can use to make Valentines for their family members. Write words and phrases on the chalkboard that students will probably use in their Valentines such as *Mom, Dad, brother, sister, Grandma, Grandpa, I love you, be mine,* and *Valentine*.

5. Have your students sit in a circle on the floor. Explain that you would like to make a sound pattern. Ask the first student to make a noise such as "beep, beep." Then ask the next student to say, "bop, bop." Have the other students take turns making one of these sounds to form a pattern. Which sound comes next? Try other sound patterns with different sounds or different numbers of sounds.

Week Two

1. The focus of this little book is finding and making patterns. Write a simple pattern on the chalkboard using shapes. Ask students to tell what comes next. Then distribute copies of page 63 and have students continue finding and making patterns.

2. Distribute copies of the little books "My Happy Family." Have students color the pages and cut them out. Help students assemble and staple their books together. Pair students with partners and have them read their little books together.

3. Read "My Happy Family" aloud to students. Have them follow along in their little books. Point to each word as you read it. After reading the story, have students look for words. Write the word *family* on the chalkboard. Ask students to find and point to the word in their books. Other words to look for are *Mommy, Daddy, sister, brother, Grandma, Grandpa, loves,* and *me*. Discuss how illustrations and pictures can help them to locate words. Have the students complete page 62 to make and design more patterns.

4. For a snack this week, have students make fruit kabob patterns on toothpicks. Fruit suggestions include grapes, pineapple, apple chunks, banana chunks, and orange segments.

My Family Lesson Plans (cont.)

Week Three

1. Have students retell the story of "My Happy Family" to check comprehension. Make up parts of the story that do not exist to see if students can correct you. Also, suggest a family member that is not in the story and determine whether or not the students can correct you. Write the story on sentence strips and post them on the chalkboard out of sequence. Have students assist you in placing the strips in order. Read the sentences again to check the sequence.

2. Create a story map of the poem with students. What happens first? What happens second? What happens last? Pair students with partners to create story maps together and have them illustrate their work. Be sure to allow time for students to share their maps with the class.

3. Read "My Happy Family" to the students from their little books or from the story chart. Now read another book about a family. (See the bibliography on page 96.) Discuss the similarities and differences between each story. Ask students if these stories are real or make-believe.

4. Read the story again with the students while they follow along in their little books. Point to each word as you read it, but this time, do not say all the words. Point to a word and have students read it. Allow students to do more and more of the reading.

5. Make patterns as a class. Ask a boy to stand, then a girl, then a boy. See if students can determine who should come next. Try a new pattern with your students based on what students are wearing. Patterns might include tennis shoes/sandals, long hair/short hair, or brown hair/black hair. When students have mastered two in a pattern, try adding three.

Week Four

1. Give each student a sheet of paper and ask the student to use crayons to design a pattern. When students have finished, have them share their patterns with partners. Compile the pages to create a class pattern book. Keep this book in the class library for student use.

2. Students can find patterns all over their world. Go on a scavenger hunt in search of patterns throughout the classroom, the school, and the outdoors. When you are finished, come back to the classroom and complete the math problems on page 64.

3. As a culminating activity for this unit, play the math games on page 65, as a class or in small groups.

Math Literacy in the Works

This page features learning-center suggestions that can be used to reinforce skills taught and discussed in the classroom. Select the centers that will best meet the needs of your students.

Math Center

- Distribute a handful of gummy bears to each of your students. Have students look at their gummy bears. How many are red? How many are yellow? How many are green? Next, have your students put these gummy bears into patterns.

- Cut out shapes (triangles, circles, squares, rectangles, and diamonds) from felt. Have the students use the shapes to make patterns on a flannel board.

- Give students a large supply of colored paperclips. Have students create necklaces or bracelets by linking the paperclips together in patterns.

- Supply students with pattern blocks and have them create patterns. Have them trace the pattern blocks and then color them. Ask students to work in pairs to begin a pattern and then have their partners finish the pattern.

Reading Center

- Write lines from "My Happy Family" on sentence strips. At this center, have students work together to read the sentences and figure out the sequence of the story. Have a little book of this story available for students to check their work.

- Set up an area in your room for independent reading. Provide large beanbags, pillows, or chairs for more comfort. For this center, have different books about families and patterns available for students. (See the bibliography on page 96.)

Writing Center

- Have paper and writing utensils available for students to make books about their families. Students should draw pictures of each of the people in their families. Bind their stories together into books by punching three holes in each page and then tying them together with yarn.

Art Center

- Set up an easel with paper. Have students use watercolors to paint patterns.

- Using sidewalk chalk, let students decorate the concrete on campus with color or shape patterns.

- Have students create colorful patterns they can eat! At this center, each student threads colored cereal Os in a pattern onto a length of yarn or licorice strings.

Making the Little Book

My Happy Family!

1

I Love Mommy,
She loves me. 2

I love Daddy,
He loves me. 3

I love Sister,
She loves me. 4

Making the Little Book *(cont.)*

I love Brother, He loves me. 5

I love Grandma, She loves me. 6

I love Grandpa, He loves me. 7

I love my family! 8

Pattern Possibilities

Patterns are fun to make. Use your crayons to make a pattern on each row of circles.

1.

2.

3.

4.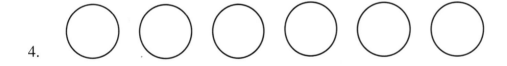

5.

6.

What Comes Next?

Find the pattern in each row. Draw the shape that comes next.

1.   _____

2.   _____

3.   _____

4. 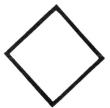 _____

5.  _____

Math in the Real World

Every day we use math. Work as a class or in small groups to solve these math problems using patterns.

---

❶ Mom was putting some flowers in a vase. First, she put in a red flower, then a yellow flower. Next, she put in a yellow flower. What color flower will she put in next?

❷ Make a pattern with shapes.

---

❸ Jenny watched a cat go in the house next door. Then she saw a dog go inside. Another cat went inside. If a simple pattern is being formed, what kind of animal will go in next?

❹ Finish the pattern. What shape comes next?

☺ △ ☺ △ ☺ _____

---

❺ Use your crayons to make a color pattern.

Fold under before reproducing.

Answers: 1. She will put in a red flower. 2. Answers will vary. 3. A dog 4. A triangle 5. Answers will vary.

64

Math Games

Games are a fun way to learn math. Play these games with partners, in groups, or as a class.

The Power of Patterns

Materials

- a deck of cards for every group

Directions

1. Divide your class into groups of three or four. Have each group shuffle the cards and place them facedown in a pile. Each player then draws five cards. The players each look at their cards and determine whether or not they can begin a pattern. A pattern can be formed by color, number, or shape. At this time, each player lays down any cards they can to form a pattern.

2. Players then take turns drawing cards to add to their patterns. Students can also play their cards on another player's pattern if they match. If a player can't play his or her cards, he or she keeps them. The first player to get rid of all of his or her cards wins.

Pattern Puzzle

Materials

- containers filled with pattern blocks (that will form a specific pattern)

Directions

1. Divide your class into groups of four or five. Give each group a container filled with pattern blocks. Have students work together as a group to determine the pattern that can be made using these pattern blocks.

2. Students must use all of the pattern blocks in their containers in order for the pattern to be correct. Students may be able to make a pattern with the pattern blocks, but it is correct only if all of the pattern blocks in the container are used.

3. When each group of students has determined the pattern, have them exchange containers with another group to see if they can solve the new puzzle.

4. As a variation of this game, have each group design a pattern using the pattern blocks. Then have groups place their pattern blocks in a container and share it with another group. The group that designed the pattern can check to make sure the other groups solved it correctly.

Hickory, Dickory, Dock

Hickory, dickory, dock!

The mouse ran up the clock;

The clock struck one,

The mouse ran down,

Hickory, dickory, dock.

Hickory, Dickory, Dock Lesson Plans

Week One

1. If possible, use a mouse puppet to read this poem. You can make a mouse puppet of your own using a paper sack or a sock. Read "Hickory, Dickory, Dock" to your class. You may copy and enlarge page 66 to use for this activity.

2. Prior to class, make the clock using the pattern on page 72. Copy this page onto cardstock so that the clock will be sturdy. Introduce the parts of the clock to your students. The parts of a clock include the numbers, the big hand (minute hand), and the little hand (hour hand). Here are the descriptions for the parts of the clock:

   • **Numbers**—The numbers on the clock represent the hours in the day.

   • **Little Hand**—The little hand on the clock points to the hour.

   • **Big Hand**—The big hand on the clock points to the minute.

   It is also important to address digital clocks. Have a digital clock plugged in to show the difference between an analog clock and a digital clock. Show students how to tell the time using both kinds of clocks.

3. Write lines of the poem on sentence strips and use a pocket chart to practice sequencing skills. As a class, place the sentence strips in order. Next, distribute the strips to students in random order. Invite students to put their sentence strips in the pocket chart in correct sequence. Place the strips and the pocket chart at your reading center for independent reading practice.

Week Two

1. The focus for this little book is telling time. Discuss the different times of day (breakfast, lunch, bedtime, morning, dinnertime, etc.). Explain that clocks help us to know what time of day it is. Make copies of page 72 on cardstock for each student. You will need to assist students with cutting out and assembling the clocks. Connect the hands to the clock using brass fasteners.

2. Once the clocks have been made, have students gather together with their clocks in hand. Holding a clock, model how to show six o'clock with the clock hands. Ask the students to move the hands on their own clocks to show six o'clock. Continue displaying different times on your clock and having the students show the same time on their clocks.

3. Read "Hickory, Dickory, Dock" aloud to students as they follow along in their little books. Model how to point to each word as you read it. After reading the story, have students look for words. Write the word *clock* on the chalkboard and ask students to locate and point to it in their books. Other words to look for are *hickory, mouse, ran, up, struck, one*, and *down*. Have students complete page 73.

Hickory, Dickory, Dock Lesson Plans *(cont.)*

Week Three

1. Have students retell the story of the mouse and the clock to check comprehension. Ask students to dramatize certain parts of the story and have classmates guess what they are doing.

2. Read "Hickory, Dickory, Dock" to the students. Next, read the complete version of "Hickory, Dickory, Dock." (See the bibliography on page 96.) Discuss the similarities and differences between each version.

3. Discuss the importance of knowing what time of day it is and what it would be like if there were no clocks. How would life be different if we never knew the time? Explain that before clocks were invented, people used the sun to tell time. Explain that the sun is located in certain parts of the sky at different times of the day.

4. Read the story again with the students while they follow along in their little books. Point to each word as you read it, but this time, do not say all the words. Point to a word without reading it and have students read it. Allow students to do more and more of the reading.

5. Play charades with your students with actions showing different times of day. Have one student at a time act out something he or she does at a particular time of day. The class guesses the time of day associated with the action. (Activities might include eating, waking up, brushing teeth, going to bed, tying shoes, getting dressed, etc.)

Week Four

1. Display several books about telling time. Allow time for students to browse through the books, gathering information from them. Students can also gather facts by listening to you read different stories about telling time everyday. Students can share their findings as oral reports, by painting murals, or in other ways you select.

2. Read another story about telling time. (See the bibliography on page 96 for suggestions, such as *Sarah's Secret Plan*.) As you read the story, frequently pause and ask students to predict what they think will happen next. Explain that making predictions can help us understand the story better. Have students complete the "Math in the Real World" activity on page 74. This activity gives students a chance to practice math and telling time.

3. If you think your students are ready, announce a time and have them display that time on their clocks. Be sure to show the correct way to display the time so students can make adjustments as needed. As a culminating activity, have students work in small groups to play the telling time games on page 75.

Math Literacy in the Works

This page features learning-center ideas that can be used to reinforce skills taught and discussed in the classroom. Select the centers that will best meet the needs of your students.

Math Center

- Using number stickers or numeral-shaped pasta, have students pick out the numbers 1 through 12. On a sheet of construction paper, have students attach the stickers or glue on pasta to make a clock. You may want to have precut arrows available for students to glue onto their clocks for hour and minutes hands.

- Place numeral-shaped pasta in a pot and provide bowls and spoons. Have each child scoop up a serving of pasta with a ladle. Then have the students identify the numbers in their bowls.

- Have an adult take students on a clock scavenger hunt, looking for all the different types of clocks they can find. Encourage them to find different kinds of clocks, such as digital clocks, alarm clocks, watches, and analog clocks.

Art Center

- Set up an easel with paper. Have students use watercolor paints to paint pictures of the mouse running up the clock. Have the students paint a large grandfather clock in their pictures.

Reading Center

- Write the lines of "Hickory, Dickory, Dock" on sentence strips. At this center, have students work together to read the sentences and determine the sequence. Display a little book of this story for student reference.

- Display all of the stories and poems about clocks and telling time for students to browse on their own. Provide chairs, large beanbags, or pillows to make the area more comfortable.

Writing Center

- Have the students make mini-books of stories about time. Have each student draw pictures of the things they do throughout the day. Have crayons available for students to illustrate their books.

Hands-On Center

- Have a variety of real clocks available for students to explore at this center. Be sure all of the clocks have been unplugged. Have students ponder these questions:

   —How do these clocks work?   —What makes an alarm clock go off?

   —What makes the ticking sound?   —How do the hands on a clock move?

Making the Little Book

Hickory, Dickory, Dock!

1

Hickory, dickory, dock!   2

The mouse ran up the clock;   3

The clock struck one,   4

Making the Little Book (cont.)

The mouse ran down,

5

Hickory, dickory, dock.

6

What time is it now?

7

The End

8

Telling Time

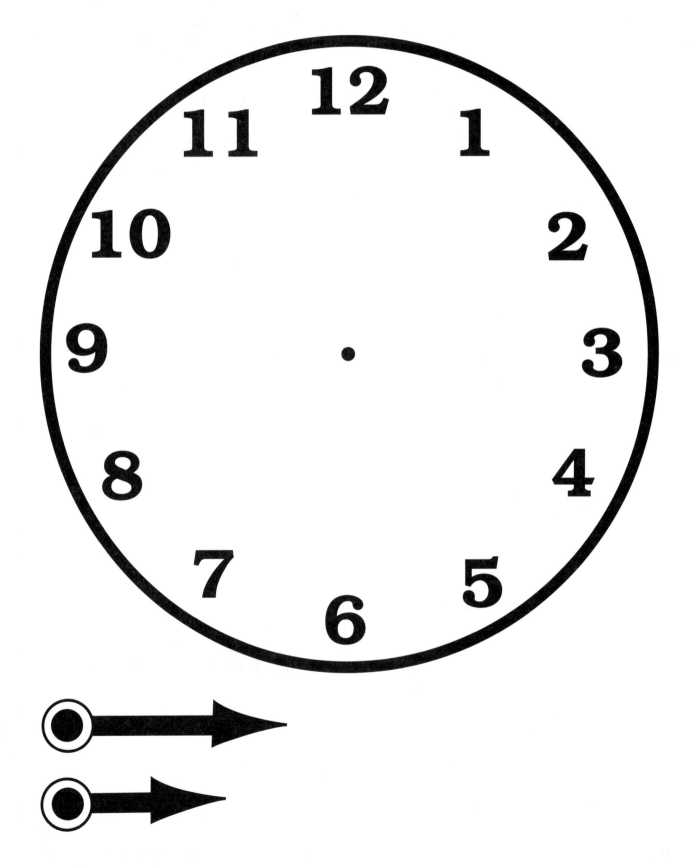

72

The Time of Day

It's morning time. The sun has just come up. Draw a picture of what you do in the morning.

It's the middle of the day. What do you do at this time? Draw a picture of what you do at noon.

It's in the afternoon. You have just come home from school. Draw a picture of what you do after school.

It's dark outside. The sun has gone to bed. Draw a picture of what you do at night.

Math in the Real World

Every day we use math. Work as a class or in small groups to solve these math problems about telling time.

❶ All of the kids are getting their lunch boxes out. They are ready to eat. What time of day is it?	**❷** What are the numbers on a clock? Write the numbers below.
❸ It's time to go to bed. What time of day is it?	**❹** In the poem, the mouse ran down when the clock struck one. What does a clock look like? Draw a clock with the hands pointing to 1:00.

❺ There are three mice on top of the barn. There is one mouse on the haystack. There is one more mouse on the tractor. How many mice are there?   Draw the number of mice.

Fold under before reproducing.

Answers: 1. It is lunch time, in the middle of the day. 2. Students will write the numbers from one to twelve. 3. It is night time, time for bed. 4. The student will draw a clock. 5. There are five mice.

Math Games

Games are a fun way to learn math. Play these games with partners, in groups, or as a class.

Keeping the Time

Materials

- timer

Directions

1. Divide your students into groups of four or five. Designate one of the students to run the timer. Select another student in the group to be first. This student chooses an action that the group will do for one minute. The student with the timer sets it for one minute.

2. Once the action has been selected, the members of the group perform the action for one minute. The student with the timer tells the group when to stop and start. Each student who is able to continue the action for one minute wins. (You may have more than one winner.)

3. To vary this game, change the duration of time. You can have students perform the selected action for ten seconds, thirty seconds, etc.

The Race for Time

Materials

- blocks, or other building materials
- watch or clock with second hand

Directions

1. Divide your class into groups of four or five. Give each group a set of blocks or other building materials. Instruct students to build a tower as high as they can in the time given. (You will keep time for this game.)

2. Be sure to vary the times that students have to build towers. For example, start off with one minute. Then move to less time. How tall can the tower get in thirty seconds? twenty seconds? fifteen seconds? ten seconds?

3. Winning towers must still be standing at the end of the designated time.

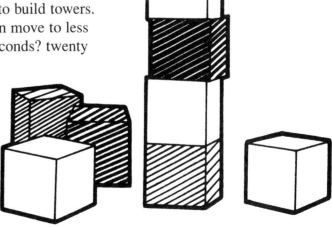

Baa, Baa, Black Sheep

Baa, baa, black sheep,

Have you any wool?

Yes sir, yes sir, three bags full.

One for my master,

One for my dame,

One for the little boy,

Who lives down the lane.

Baa, baa, black sheep,

Have you any wool?

Yes sir, yes sir, three bags full.

Baa, Baa, Black Sheep Lesson Plans

Week One

1. Ask students questions about sheep.
   - What is sheep wool?
   - What does sheep wool feel like?
   - What do people do with sheep wool?
   - Have they ever seen someone spinning or weaving wool?

   If possible, have samples of wool available for students to feel. Read the poem "Baa, Baa, Black Sheep." You may copy and enlarge page 76 to use for this activity.

2. Ask students why the master, the dame, and the little boy in the poem would want bags of wool. What can be done with wool? Hold up several pieces of clothing made of wool and ask students to guess what these clothes are made of. Point out that these clothes are made of the wool from sheep.

3. Prior to reading the poem again, use a cloze technique by covering several words in the poem. Ask students to read the poem and name the missing words. Move pieces of paper and cover up different words to see if your students can fill in the covered words. If time allows, have students use adhesive notes to cover up words in the poem for other students to discover.

Week Two

1. The focus of this little book is addition. Discuss with the children how to add. Show them simple addition problems using students as part of the problem. Ask two students to stand at one end of the room. Ask one student to stand at the other end of the room. Ask students, "If you were to combine both groups of students, how many would there be?" Do more of these types of addition problems. Distribute copies of page 82 for students. This page will give students more practice with adding groups.

2. Distribute copies of the little book "Baa, Baa, Black Sheep." Have students color the pages and cut them out. Help them to assemble and staple their books together. Pair students with partners and have them read their little books together. You can use a variety of methods to read the little book with your students.

3. Read "Baa, Baa Black Sheep" aloud to students as they follow along in their little books. Model how to point to each word as you read it. After reading the story, have students look for words. Write the word *wool* on the chalkboard and ask students to find and point to the word. Other words to look for are *black, sheep, have, yes, sir, three, bags, full,* and *master.*

4. Instruct students to look in their little books to find the addition problem in the poem. Read through the poem one page at a time. Draw a picture of each of the bags of wool and instruct students to count the bags and determine the total. Have students complete page 83 for more addition practice.

Baa, Baa, Black Sheep Lesson Plans *(cont.)*

Week Three

1. Read "Baa, Baa, Black Sheep" to the students. Now read a different story about sheep. Compare the story and the rhyme. (See the bibliography on page 96.)

2. Write each line of the poem on a different sentence strip. Post the sentence strips in random order on the chalkboard. Have students assist you in placing the strips in order. Read through the sentences again to check the sequence. Make changes as needed.

3. Read the story again with the students while they follow along in their little books. Point to each word as you read it, but do not say all the words. Point to a word without reading it and have students read it. Allow students to do more reading.

4. As an art activity, have students make sheep by gluing cotton balls onto construction paper. Post the sheep around the room.

Week Four

1. Have several nonfiction books about sheep and other farm animals available. Allow time for students to browse through the books and gather as much information as they can. Have them share their findings with the class. Make a list of the facts they found. Lead a discussion with students about things we are able to get from sheep.

2. On the chalkboard write "Sheep wool is…." Then have each student copy these words and write an ending to the sentence. Remind students to put a period at the end of the sentence. Provide crayons or colored pencils and have students illustrate their sentences. Allow students to share their work with one another. Bind student pages together to create a book to display in the class library.

3. Discuss with students the types of animals that live on a farm. Sing the song, "Old MacDonald Had a Farm" with students. Each time a farm animal is mentioned, write or draw a picture of it on the chalkboard. When the song is finished, ask the students how many farm animals Old MacDonald has. Point to each animal name or picture as you count it. Have students complete the "Math in the Real World" activity on page 84. This page gives students practice with addition.

4. Have students review addition by using their fingers. Have students hold up a certain number of fingers on one hand. Then instruct students to hold up a certain number of fingers on the other hand. Show students how to add the fingers all together. Do more practice with addition by creating addition story problems using your students names. Encourage students to create story problems of their own using classmates' names.

5. Help students make an addition book. Cut and staple five pieces of paper together to make a little book with ten pages. On each page, a student draws two sets of pictures to add together. The student then writes the numeral that represents' the total number of objects. As a concluding activity for this unit, play the games on page 85.

Math Literacy in the Works

This page features learning-center suggestions that can be used to reinforce skills taught. Select the centers that will best meet the needs of your students.

Math Center

- Have salt dough available for students to make sets of objects. Instruct students to add the sets of objects together to practice addition.

- Select a number on which to focus. Have students come up with as many different ways as they can to write addition sentences that add up to that number. You might want to have them use manipulatives.

Reading Center

- Write each line of "Baa, Baa, Black Sheep" on a different sentence strip. At this center, have students work together to read the sentences and determine the correct sequence. Have a little book of the poem available for students to check their work.

- Display nonfiction books, magazine articles, and posters about farm animals. Have students browse these materials to learn more about farm animals. Arrange a time in the day to have students report to the class what they have learned about farm animals.

- Set up an area in your room for independent reading. Provide large beanbags, pillows, or chairs for more comfort. Keep a shelf of books available at all times for students to read and browse. For this center, have versions of poems and nursery rhymes available for students to read. Be sure that "Baa, Baa, Black Sheep" is featured in one of these books. (See the bibiography on page 96 for suggestions.)

Art Center

- Have students color pictures of things they could make out of wool. When they have finished, cut the pictures into large puzzle pieces. Students can then try to put their puzzles back together again. Store the puzzles in an envelope so the pieces won't get lost.

Dramatic Play Center

- Provide simple instruments for students to create a beat as they read or recite "Baa, Baa Black Sheep." The students could tap spoons together, beat on empty containers, shake small containers of rice and beans, etc.

Writing Center

- Make mini-books for students to write their own stories about farm animals. Allow students to use farm animal stencils or cutouts to assist with their illustrations.

Making the Little Book

Baa, Baa, Black Sheep

1

Baa, Baa, black sheep,

2

have you any wool?

3

Yes, sir, yes, sir, three bags full.

4

Making the Little Book *(cont.)*

**One for my master,
One for my dame,**   5

**One for the little
boy who lives
down the lane.**   6

**Baa, baa, black
sheep, have you any
wool?**   7

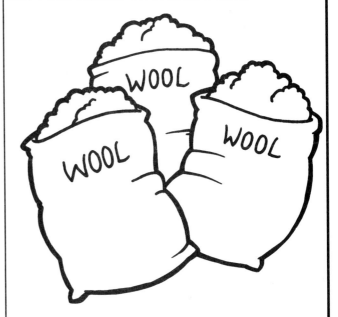

**Yes sir, yes sir,
three bags full.**   8

Adding It All Up!

Add the groups of animals. Write the number in the box.

1. +  =

2.  + =

3.  + =

4. + 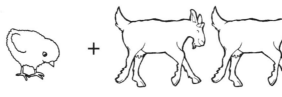 =

5.  +  =

6. +  =

82

Addition Sentences

Try adding with numbers. The first one has been done for you.

1. 2 + 3 = _____5_____

2. 2 + 2 = _____

3. 1 + 1 = _____

4. 0 + 2 = _____

5. 1 + 3 = _____

6. 2 + 4 = _____

Math in the Real World

Every day we use math. Work as a class or in small groups to solve these addition math problems.

❶ Old MacDonald has three chickens and two cows. How many animals does he have in all?	**❷** On this farm, there are six horses and one pony. How many are there in all?
❸ Old MacDonald has three black sheep and four white sheep. How many sheep does he have in all?	**❹** If the black sheep gives a bag to the master, his dame, and the little boy who lives down the lane, how many bags does the sheep give in all?

❺ There is a cat in the barn, a cat in the field, and a cat under the tractor. How many cats are there? Draw the number of cats.

Fold under before reproducing.

Answers: 1. There are five. 2. There are seven. 3. There are seven sheep. 4. The sheep gives three bags. 5. There are three cats.

Math Games

Games are a fun way to learn math. Play these games with partners, in groups, or as a class.

On the Farm!

Materials

- paper bags
- marker
- plastic farm animals

Directions

1. Begin by writing a different number on the outside of each paper bag.

2. Divide your class into two groups. One group will be the animal group and one will be the basket group.

3. Give each student in the basket group a paper bag.

4. Next, give a handful of plastic farm animals to each student in the animal group.

5. The students with the bags try to get the corresponding number of animals in their bags. The students with the animals can only give out one or two animals at a time. After all students with bags have filled them with the correct amount of animals, switch roles and play again.

Stick to It!

Materials

- paper
- stickers of farm animals

Directions

1. Distribute a sheet of paper to each student. Explain that they are to create addition pictures using farm animal stickers. Each student selects a small number of stickers to put on one side of the addition problem and a different set of stickers to put on the other side. The student counts all the stickers in both groups and writes the number.

   Example:

   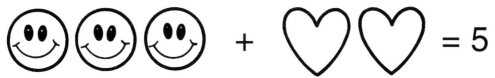

2. Vary the above activity by having one student attach a group of stickers to the paper. Then this student gives his or her paper to another student to select the number of stickers for the second group. The first student adds up all the stickers and writes the answer.

Five Little Monkeys

Five little monkeys jumping on the bed,
One fell off and bumped his head,

(chorus)

Mama called the doctor and the doctor said,
"No more monkeys jumping on the bed!"

Four little monkeys jumping on the bed.
One fell off and bumped his head.

Repeat chorus.

Three little monkeys jumping on the bed,
One fell off and bumped his head.

Repeat chorus.

Two little monkeys jumping on the bed,
One fell off and bumped his head.

Repeat chorus.

One little monkey jumping on the bed,

One fell off and bumped his head.

Repeat chorus.

86

Five Little Monkeys Lesson Plans

Week One

1. Ask students to tell you about their favorite wild animals. Where do they live? What do they eat? Have they ever seen these animals in real life? Where? How are wild animals different from house pets? What other facts do they know about these animals?

2. Make a copy of the poem on page 86. Read and discuss "Five Little Monkeys." Ask questions such as:

   - What are the monkeys doing?
   - What happens to the number of monkeys jumping on the bed?
   - Is this poem real or make-believe? How can you tell?

3. Read the poem again, but this time substitute the name of a different animal. Read the poem several more times using a different animal each time.

4. Explain that learning to subtract is important. In this poem about monkeys, subtraction is used. Each time a monkey falls off the bed, the number of monkeys gets smaller. Make up a subtraction word problem using the students names and ask the class to solve the problem.

5. Next, enlist the help of your students to make up more subtraction problems using wild animals. Working as a class, read and solve the subtraction problems on page 92.

Week Two

1. Distribute copies of the "Five Little Monkeys" little book. Have students color the pages and cut them out. Help students assemble and staple their books together. Pair students with partners and have them read their little books together.

2. Read "Five Little Monkeys" aloud to students. Have students follow along in their little books, pointing to each word as you read it. After reading the story, have students look for words. Write the word *monkey* on the chalkboard and ask students to find it. Other words to look for are *five, four, three, two, one, jumping, bed, off, head, bumped,* and *fell.* Discuss how illustrations and pictures can help with locating words. Have students complete page 93.

3. Discuss wild animals with your students. If possible, display pictures of wild animals in their natural habitats. With student help, make a list on the chalkboard of wild animals. Ask what the animals have in common? What makes them different? What do they need in order to survive? How can we learn more about wild animals?

Five Little Monkeys Lesson Plans *(cont.)*

Week Three

1. Have students retell the poem about the monkeys to check comprehension. Make up fictional statements about the poem to determine whether or not students can correct you.

2. Invite someone who works with wild animals or has knowledge about wild animals to speak with your class.

3. Read "Five Little Monkeys." Ask students to tell you word-for-word the lines from the poem. Write their responses on the chalkboard. Next, hold up a poster with the words of this poem on it and check student work. Were the lines and words in correct order? Make changes as needed. Talk with students about story or poem details. The details of a story or poem can help aid comprehension.

4. Read the poem again with the students while they follow along in their little books. Point to each word as you read it, but do not say all of the words. Point to a word without reading it and have students read it. Allow students to do more and more of the reading.

5. As an art activity, have each student make a paper bag puppet of a wild animal. With the help of an adult, the student designs the face of the puppet on the bottom flap of the bag. The student should color the face using markers or paint. Colored yarn can be used to add hair, fur, or a mane. Let the puppet dry completely before using. When all students' puppets are dry, have them use the puppets to act out math problems.

Week Four

1. Read other stories with your class about monkeys and wild animals. You can refer to the bibliography on page 96 for suggestions. Discuss your findings as a class.

2. Read "Five Little Monkeys" again. Ask the students, "What happened next?" Encourage them to brainstorm what might happen next after the end of the poem. What happens to the five monkeys? Have students illustrate their new endings. You can record their dictations.

3. Have students review subtraction using their fingers. Have them hold up a certain number of fingers on one hand. Then instruct them to select a number to take away. Have the student put this number of fingers down. How many are left?

4. As a culminating activity, have students play the games on page 95. These games will reinforce subtraction skills.

Math Literacy in the Works

This page features learning-center suggestions that can be used to reinforce skills taught. Select the centers that will best meet the needs of your students.

Math Center

- On a sheet of paper, have a student use watercolors to paint the following: five zebras, four lions, three giraffes, two monkeys, and one snake. Be sure to have a picture of each type of wild animal available for students to use as a reference.

- Have connectable plastic cubes available for students to practice subtraction. Have them connect certain numbers of cubes. Then have the students take some away and count the remainder.

Writing Center

- Ask questions, such as:

  —What are the monkeys like in this little book?

  —What words can be used to describe them?

  —How would you describe yourself?

  —Are you like the monkeys?

- Have each student draw a self-portrait. Ask the students to write describing words to describe themselves.

- Have students write stories about the monkeys in the poem. Have them draw pictures of the monkeys at school, in the store, or at the park. How would the monkeys behave? Assist them, as needed, with words and sentences to accompany the pictures.

Reading Center

- Write each line of the poem on a different sentence strip. At this center, have students work together to read the sentences and determine the correct sequence. Have a little book of this poem available for students to check their work.

- Set up an area in your room for independent reading. Provide large beanbags, pillows, or chairs for more comfort. Keep a shelf of books about wild animals available for students to read and compare. (See the bibliography on page 96 for suggestions.)

Art Center

- Using old magazines and coloring books, have students cut out pictures of wild animals and their environments. Then give each student a piece of construction paper to fold in half. Each student pastes pictures of things that represent wild animals on one side. On the other side, the student pastes magazine pictures of things from their own lives. How are these things different? How are they the same?

Dramatic Play Center

- Have students work in groups of five to reenact the poem about the five little monkeys. Place a blanket on the floor for each group to use as a bed. Remind the students to play safely and only pretend to bump their heads.

Five Little Monkeys

1

Five little monkeys jumping on the bed, one fell off and bumped his head.   2

Four little monkeys jumping on the bed, one fell off and bumped his head.   3

Three little monkeys jumping on the bed, one fell off and bumped his head.   4

Making the Little Book *(cont.)*

Two little monkeys jumping on the bed, one fell off and bumped his head.   5

One little monkey jumping on the bed, one fell off and bumped his head.   6

Mama called the doctor and the doctor said,   7

"No more monkeys jumping on the bed!" 8

Subtraction

Subtraction means taking away. Look at each of the math problems below. How many are left after you take some away? Draw a picture that shows the math problem.

1. 3 – 2 = _____

2. 2 – 2 = _____

3. 4 – 1 = _____

4. 5 – 2 = _____

5. 2 – 1 = _____

Taking Away

Look at the pictures in each row. Cross out some of the pictures. Write the number in the box to show how many are left.

1.

2.

3.

4.

5.

#3713 A Year of Themes: Math

Math in the Real World

Every day we use math. Work as a class or in small groups to solve these subtraction math problems.

❶ Five tigers were lying in the sun. Two got up and moved to a different place. How many tigers were left?	**❷** Seven zebras were eating their dinner. A lion came up and scared them all away. How many were left?
❸ Draw a picture of three snakes. Cross out two of your snakes. How many are left?	**❹** There were five monkeys jumping on the bed. Two fell off and bumped their heads. How many were left jumping?

❺ Five giraffes were eating leaves from a tree. One giraffe got tired and went to rest. How many giraffes were left at the tree eating? Draw the number of giraffes left.

Fold under before reproducing.

Answers: 1. Three tigers were left. 2. Zero. No zebras were left. 3. One snake is left. 4. Three monkeys were left. 5. Four giraffes were left.

Math Games

Games are a fun way to learn math. Play these games with partners, in groups, or as a class.

Remove it First!

Materials

- string to thread the beads
- wooden beads
- four dice

Directions

1. Divide your class into groups of four. Give each student a string with a knot tied at one end. Give each group a die and a bucket of beads.

2. Have students thread beads on their strings to form a necklace. (Students can make patterns with their beads, if desired.) Ask the students to count their beads. They should all have the same number of beads on their strings. Do not tie the string together.

3. Next, have the students take turns rolling the die. The student counts the dots on the die to see how many beads to take off his or her string. The object of the game is to be the first person to take off all of his or her beads.

Give it a Spin!

Materials

- spinner with the numbers 0, 1, 2, 3
- uncooked noodles
- small bowls

Directions

1. Prior to playing this game, make a spinner out of cardstock. In the center, attach a brass fastener. Then hook a paper clip around the brass fastener to make the spinner. Divide the spinner into four parts. Write the numbers 0, 1, 2, and 3 on the spinner.

2. Divide your class into groups of three or four. Give each group a bowl full of noodles and a spinner. Each student takes a turn spinning the spinner. The student takes that number of noodles out of the bowl. Then the student spins the spinner again. This time, the student puts some noodles back in the bowl. How many are left?

3. As a variation, each student begins with ten noodles. Each player takes a turn spinning the spinner. He or she must take that many noodles away. Play continues in this manner until someone has lost all of his or her noodles. This player is the winner!

Bibliography

Fiction

Adams, Pam. *Old MacDonald Had a Farm.* Child's Play Int'l, 1999.

Aylesworth, Jim. *The Completed Hickory Dickory Dock.* Atheneum, 1990.

Brett, Jan. *Annie and the Wild Animals.* Houghton Mifflin Co, 1989.

Christelow, Eileen. *Five Little Monkeys Jumping on the Bed.* Scott Foresman, 1990.

———. *Five Little Monkeys Sitting in a Tree.* Houghton Mifflin, 1999.

———. *Five Little Monkeys Wash the Car.* Houghton Mifflin, 2000.

Collins, Heather. *One, Two, Buckle My Shoe.* Kids Can Press, 1997.

Cronin, Doreen. *Giggle, Giggle, Quack.* Simon and Schuster, 2002.

Eastman, P.D. *Are You My Mother?* Random House, 1960.

Edwards, Linda. *One, Two, Buckle My Shoe.* Usborne Pub Ltd, 2002.

Esphyr Slobodkina. *Caps for Sale.* Harper Trophy, 1987.

Johns, Linda. *Sarah's Secret Plan.* Troll, 1995.

Low, Joseph. *Mice Twice.* Aladdin, 1986.

McCafferty, Catherine. *Picture Me and My Grandma.* Picture Me Books, 1998.

Moroney, Tracey. *One, Two, Buckle My Shoe.* Reader's Digest Children's Books, 1997.

Schwartz, David. *How Much is a Million?* Mulberry Books, 1993.

Siddalls, Mary McKenna. *Millions of Snowflakes.* Clarion Books, 1998.

Silverman, Erica. *Big Pumpkin.* Aladdin Paperbacks, 1995.

Slawson, Michele Benoit. *Apple Picking Time.* Dragonfly, 1998.

Van Rynbach, Iris. *Five Little Pumpkins.* Boyd Mills, 1995.

White, Linda. *Too Many Pumpkins.* Holiday House, 1997.

Nonfiction

Bang, Molly Garrett. *Ten, Nine, Eight.* Tupelo Books, 1998.

Carter, David A. *How Many Bugs in a Box?* Little Simon, 1988.

Fowler, Alan. *It's a Fruit, It's a Vegetable, It's a Pumpkin.* Children's Press, 1996.

Hoban, Tana. *Shapes, Shapes, Shapes.* Scott Foresman, 1996.

Hutchings, Amy. *Picking Apples and Pumpkins.* Cartwheel Books, 1994.

Kurtz, Shirley. *Applesauce.* Good Books, 1992.

Levenson, George. *Pumpkin Circle: The Story of a Garden.* Tricyle Press, 2002.

Maestro, Betsy. *How Do Apples Grow?* Harper Trophy, 1993.

Martin, Jacqueline Biggs. *Snowflake Bentley.* Houghton Mifflin Co., 1998.

Nilsen, Anna. *I Can Add.* Larousse Kingfisher Chambers, 2000.

———. *I Can Count 1 to 10.* Larousse Kingfisher Chambers, 1999.

———. *I Can Subtract.* Larousse Kingfisher Chambers, 2000.

Seuss, Dr. *One Fish, Two Fish, Red Fish, Blue Fish.* Random House, 1981.

Thong, Roseanne. *Round is a Moon Cake: Book of Shapes.* Chronicle Books, 2000.

Walker, Sarah. *Eye Wonder: Big Cats.* Dorling Kindersley, 2002.